2972 3706

4/04

Beautiful America's
Montana

Beautiful America's
Montana

Photography by
Gordon and Cathie Sullivan

Text by Linda Stirling

Beautiful America Publishing Company

Front cover: Bullhead Lake, Glacier National Park

Opposite title page: St. Mary Lake and Triple Arches, Glacier National Park

Published by
Beautiful America Publishing Company
P.O. Box 244
Woodburn, OR 97071

Library of Congress Catalog Number 00-037960

ISBN 0-89802-725-X
ISBN 0-89802-724-1 (paperback)

Printed in Korea

Contents

Mount Gould, Glacier National Park

Montana black bear

Rising Wolf Mountain, Glacier National Park

Introduction

Ask any schoolchild about Montana and they will likely toss at you textbook descriptions of mountains and wilderness, open spaces, and wildlife. And they'd be right, but they'd only be touching upon a fraction of the vastness and variety of this state. Montana is a dream come true for the explorer and nature-lover, a place where you can still go for a week without seeing another person, or where you can jump into the hustle and excitement of a booming city. As the nation's fourth largest state, Montana covers 147,046 square miles and is bordered by four states and three Canadian provinces. On average, Montana measures 550 miles from east to west and 275 miles from north to south. The highest point in Montana is 12,799-foot Granite Peak in the Beartooth Range, and the lowest point is where the Kootenai River enters Idaho at an elevation of 1,820 feet. For all the space and scenery, Montana is comparatively uncrowded.

While the name Montana comes from a Spanish word that means "mountainous" the eastern three-fifths is plains country. Walter P. Webb, who wrote *The West and the Desert* in 1958 described it as "the burnt right flank of the desert." The western two-fifths is dominated by the Rockies and their kindred, 25 or so ranges cluster 'round. The Continental Divide also makes its appearance for a bit, forming the general north-south boundary between Montana and her western neighbor. What you get when you toss all this together is a unique watershed that drains into three different oceans. From their birth in Glacier National Park and in Teton County streams flow, via the Belly, the St. Mary's and the Waterton, across Canada and ultimately into the Hudson Bay and the Arctic Ocean. From Butte, the Clark Fork gathers the waters of the Blackfoot, the Bitterroot and the Flathead, among others, and winds toward the Pacific Ocean. The Missouri, the early highroad to the frontier, appears in southwestern Montana and journeys to the Gulf of Mexico. At Triple Divide Peak in Glacier National Park streams flow not only east and west but also north to Hudson Bay. From this mix of rivers, mountains, and plains, you get beauty. Fabulous beauty!

And beauty at its most raw. Seventy-below zero was recorded in Roger's Pass, northwest of Helena, and 117 degrees above zero at Glendive and Medicine Lake; snow can reach depths of 300 inches in some years; some claim the wind in the Madison Valley blows four ways at once. The weather won't deter you, though. One glimpse of Montana's offerings and you'll itch to see more. It's the kind of scenery that draws you with a primal pull.

History

Two groups of Native Americans were among the first settlers in this land. They were from the Great Plains' group, which included the Blackfoot, Flathead, and Crow people, and from the Rocky Mountain Region Native Americans, which included the Salish and the Kootenai. In the 18th century, France may have had trappers venturing into Montana, or so it was claimed, although the area was largely unexplored. In 1803, the United States, through the Louisiana Purchase acquired the territory from France. President Thomas Jefferson decided to send the Lewis and Clark Expedition to explore the land and to search for a water route to the Pacific Ocean. The expedition included: 29 white men; York, who was a black servant to Clark; a Shosone Indian girl named Sacajawea; her baby; and Scammon, one of the few dogs who made a name for themselves in history. Because the Louisiana Purchase had been bought sight unseen, President Jefferson thought it wise to send his secretary, Meriwether Lewis, and an Army officer, William Clark to look after the purchase. The expedition took off from St. Louis, Missouri on May 14, 1804 and returned on September 23, 1806 after traveling 4,000 miles. More than half of the winding miles covered were in Montana.

Lewis and Clark found the headwaters of the great Missouri River, three rivers that they called The Jefferson, after the president; the Gallatin, for Albert Gallatin, secretary of the treasury; and the Madison, for James Madison, secretary of state. Lewis named Maria's River (which has become Marias) for his cousin, Maria Wood. Clark named the Judith River for a woman he knew. He apparently was love-smitten but didn't really know the woman well, for he later discovered her name to be Julia. She apparently forgave him the slip, for he married her after he returned from the journey.

Even Sacajawea's little one had a landmark named for him, Pompey's Pillar. The "pillar" is a flat-topped rock in the Yellowstone Valley that still bears the carved words, "Wm. Clark, July 25, 1806."

Great Falls, where it took the expedition 26 days to portage around the falls, is where the city of Great Falls now lies.

The Indians were fascinated by York, the black member of the troop. They flocked around him, admiring and curious. They had seen a few white men, but never a black man. After the expedition was over, York returned to this wilderness and became a chief in one of the tribes.

One of the primary requests Jefferson made was for the expedition to find out whether or not there

Wanless Lake, Cabinet Mountains Wilderness

Opposite: Heaven's Peak, Glacier National Park

was a Northwest Passage, a water route through all those mountains. But the expedition couldn't find any navigable rivers in the Rockies and had to buy horses from the Shoshone Indians. This in itself proved to be a challenge, as the poor Indians were scared out of their wits to see these interlopers. Once the explorers caught up with them, Sacajawea, who not only spoke the language, but whose brother was chief of the tribe, was able to get the Indians to work with them. Although the explorers nearly starved as they crossed the Rockies, they did find a river that flowed into the Columbia. Once there, they built boats and went on to the Pacific Ocean.

Riding hard on the heels of the explorers were fur traders and trappers. The first building in Montana was built by Manuel Lisa who built a trading post where the Bighorn River flows into the Yellowstone. The trappers didn't contribute anything to Montana except some great stories of valor and endurance. One of the trappers, John Coulter, who came with Lewis and Clark and stayed because he liked the wilderness, told of a land where steam spurted up from the ground. That gave the other trappers a good laugh until the place they laughingly called "Coulter's Hell" turned out to be just as he described. We know it now, of course, as Yellowstone National Park.

Once people grew tired of the fashion of furs, Montana dipped in popularity. The roaming trappers moved on and mostly abandoned the state. The first travelers who came with the intention of staying and building permanent structures were the "black robes" as the Indians called the missionaries. The leader of this first group was Father Pierre Jean De Smet, a Belgian. Father De Smet, two other missionaries, and three lay brothers constructed the first church, made of logs, in the beautiful Bitterroot Valley.

At this time most people who were looking for homes "out West" were traveling in covered wagons to California or the Oregon country. They went south, through Wyoming, along the Oregon Trail. Montana's mountains were just an obstacle . . . at least until gold was found. In 1862, wandering prospectors found gold in Grasshopper Creek. The move to Montana was on.

Grasshopper Creek spawned the town of Bannack, which was named for the Bannock Indians. Nobody worried about the spelling. A man with a shovel could dig placer gold right out of the ground, then wash the dirt and gravel away in the stream. It was a dream for any poor man with a good back. In one of the quickly thrown together saloons, one customer brought about the definition of "pay dirt." He'd tromped in with so much mud on his boots, his buddies joked that there was probably a lot of gold on his shoes. They decided to scrape off the mud and wash it . . . and recovered $5 worth of gold.

During the first year of gold digging at Grasshopper Creek — and remember this was 1862 — the mines produced $5 million in gold dust and nuggets. This same kind of mineral richness brought about the development of other Montana towns. Before the gold rush, there were only a few hundred non-Indian inhabitants. Within a year, there were about 15,000 new inhabitants. With them came the need for government.

A smooth-talking, gun-slinging man named Henry Plummer got into a fight with the first sheriff, Henry Crawford. Crawford shot Plummer in the arm, but when Crawford left Montana forever, Plummer was elected sheriff to fill his shoes. Unbeknownst at the time was Plummer's lurid past — he had left a trail of dead men behind him in the mining camps of California and Idaho.

Plummer headed a band of about 50 thieves and murderers. They had dubbed themselves, the Innocents, but other people, in whispers, called them road agents. Plummer's deputies were villains, too . . . all but one. The others shot the sole honest deputy down and went unpunished for their crime. More than a hundred men were killed or disappeared because of Plummer and his crew. Finally, after a brutal killing just before Christmas in 1863, a group of angry businessmen and miners rounded up several suspects, held a public trial, and hanged one of the guilty men. Two dozen of the solid citizens then met secretly and formed a committee of vigilance. Though not sanctioned under the law, they rode hard and fast to track down the road agents. In six weeks time they captured, tried, and executed 26 of the road agents, including Sheriff John Plummer.

One of the mysteries that remains from this time is the use of the numbers 3-7-77 that were left as warning for the outlaws. Some people say they signified the dimensions of a grave: 3 feet wide, 7 feet long, and 77 inches deep. Whatever the meaning the warning was clear: leave town or die.

In 1864, Montana got its present boundaries, its name, and a legal government when Congress made it a state. Virginia City was made the capital, but in 1875, the capital was moved to Helena.

With more and more white settlers arriving in Montana, conflicts arose with the native population. The natives had tried reasoning with the white men on what became the Bozeman Trail. In 1863, John Bozeman and his wagon train met up with 150 Sioux and Cheyennes — many more than were in Bozeman's traveling party. The old chief gave Bozeman and his partners a message that was calm and clear.

Johnson Lake, Anaconda-Pintler Wilderness

Autumn at the Blackfoot River near Helmsville

You can't go on in the direction you are going. You are going into our country, where we hunt. This is the only good big hunting ground left for us. Your people have taken the rest or scared the game away.

We won't let our women and children starve. This is where we take meat, and we will keep this land.

Along the great road to the south, white men have driven away all the buffalo and antelope. We won't let you do that here.

If you will turn back to the Platte, we will let you go. We will not hurt you. But if you go on into our hunting country, our people will wipe you out. They have already been warned with signal fires on the mountains.

Bozeman withdrew just enough to try to gain assistance from the Army. Historical letters from Major Thomas L. Mackey, commanding officer at Fort Laramie, show what he thought of Bozeman's attempt:

I understand that a treaty exists with the Indians reserving the Country North of the Platte to them as a hunting ground, and especially stipulating that no highway should be made through this Country. This route these emigrants have taken runs directly through this reservation. When this train was about ready to leave Deer Creek on this trip they were told by some Indians of the existence of this treaty and warned not to attempt it as they would not be permitted to go through.

Learning these facts I telegraphed Lt. Love, commanding at Deer Creek, not to let them move in that direction. Several dispatches passed between myself and the leaders of this train, in reference to the matter and they were so urgent in their request to be permitted to go through on this route that I finally recalled the order to Lt. Love at the same time telling these men that if they went over this route they did so at their own peril.

Under these circumstances they having been repeatedly warned and finally got into trouble on account of their own willfulness. I think they should be brought back to the old road and not sent through.

Bozeman persisted, taking wagon train after wagon train through, and makeshift graves multiplied along the Bozeman trail before it was eventually shut down in 1868.

After the closing of Bozeman, the Sioux were promised a much larger hunting ground in the Black Hills. The discovery of gold there brought about the destruction of that promise. The government vainly attempted to keep the gold seekers out, finally giving up on the effort and opening the treaty lands to

Mount Reynolds, Glacier National Park

miners who were willing to take the risk. Prospectors poured into the Black Hills by the thousands. When young Indian braves slipped off to join non-treaty Indians, authorities ordered them back, despite the government treaties that allowed them to hunt. Both Sitting Bull and Crazy Horse refused to be ordered about by the government in this way. The "problem Indians" were dumped in the lap of the Army in the spring of 1876. Crazy Horse, called the "bravest of the brave" by both Indians and non-natives, allied with Sitting Bull, who was a combination medicine-man warrior. They harassed the whites on the Bozeman Road as well as those who surveyed for the Union Pacific Railroad. Crazy Horse had also fought a series of battles with Lt. Colonel George Custer in the Yellowstone Valley. Finally, in 1876, three military groups moved against the Sioux and their Northern Cheyenne allies. The first column was under the command of General George Crook, and it moved north from Fort Fetterman; the second was led by Colonel John Gibbon who came east from Fort Ellis; and the third, commanded by General Alfred Terry, started west from Fort Abraham Lincoln below Bismark, North Dakota. Part of Terry's command was led by the man the Sioux called "the Chief of all the Thieves," Lt. Colonel Custer. Custer was sent south along the Rosebud to prevent the Indians from retreating into the Bighorns. Impatient, Custer moved too soon and the Indians attacked killing 264 of his men. Even with this Indian success, the Indians were eventually forced back to their reservations. There were many more skirmishes, with the Indians always forced back even further.

One has to sympathize with the Indians who had tried to get along with the white men who came to their lands. Their lives were closely tied to the health of the land and its animals, especially the comings and goings of the great buffalo herds, so it was no wonder the Indians were adamant about the white man staying out of their hunting areas.

State Parks by Country

While Montana has her world-famous national parks, her state parks provide unequaled opportunities to experience another side of the history and the beauty of this country. Dozens of state parks are worthy of exploration. The Montana Fish Wildlife and Parks and the tourism division divide the state into "countries." They are dubbed Glacier Country, Gold West Country, Yellowstone Country, Charlie Russell Country, Missouri River Country, and Custer Country.

Missouri River Country

This is a land of fascinating high plains and deep badlands, vast wheat ranches, and the wonderful Missouri River. Located in Montana's northeast corner, it is home to a million-acre wildlife refuge and to Fort Peck Lake, which is one of the nation's best walleye and sauger fisheries. The largest state park here is Hell Creek. Camping, swimming, canoeing and boating are all offered at this park, which is a launching point to the vast and rugged Missouri Breaks area.

Russell Country

Russell Country is named after the famed western artist, Charlie Russell. Here you can float the wild and scenic Missouri River, visit prehistoric hunting sites, explore the mountain ranges where the Great Plains meet the Rockies, or travel along the Lewis and Clark Trail.

Giant Springs Heritage State Park, discovered by Lewis and Clark in 1805, is the home of one of the largest freshwater springs in the world. It is also the site of the Roe River, which, along with the D River in Oregon, lays claim to be the world's shortest river. Giant Springs flows at 7.9 million gallons per hour at a constant temperature of 54 degrees. Each year, more than 250,000 people visit to see the springs, picnic on the banks of the Missouri River, see Rainbow Falls Overlook, or to view the variety of bird life. The park is just east of the town of Great Falls. Popular River's Edge Trail also runs through the park.

Beautiful Lake McDonald, Glacier National Park

Bird Woman Falls, Glacier National Park

A 61-mile float trip is possible down the remote and beautiful Smith River Canyon. Twenty-seven boat camps line the wild river from Camp Baker to the take-out point at Eden Bridge. Reservations and permits are needed before floating the river. Every effort is made by the state to preserve the wonder of this river. It is truly one of the most breathtaking spots in Montana, indeed in the world.

Ackley Lake is another beautiful spot within Russell Country with campgrounds, fishing, boating and swimming all available.

If you love remote ghost towns, a primitive trail follows an abandoned railroad grade through the scenic Belt Creek Gorge. There are plenty of stream fishing opportunities along the way, and, fishing or not, you'll have to cross the creek, so make sure you're exploring at a time of year when the water is low. You will ultimately reach Sluice Boxes, an undeveloped park.

Glacier Country

Montana's dazzling northwest corner offers the ultimate in wilderness, wildlife, lakes and forests. Glacier National Park has all the name recognition, but don't forget parks like Council Grove, just outside Missoula. Though only a day-use park, this dip into history preserves where the Hellgate treaty was signed, an 1855 council between Isaac Stevens, the Flathead Kootenai and the Pend d'Oreille Indians.

Canadian geese watchers as well as those headed for Whitehorse Island find Big Arm Unit, located on Flathead Lake's Big Arm Bay to be an enjoyable park. Flathead Lake, a stunning lake located between Kalispell and Polson, is the largest freshwater lake west of the Mississippi River. Dredged by receding glaciers about 12,000 years ago, the lake is 28 miles long and varies between 5 and 15 miles wide, with 185 miles of shoreline. Flathead Lake is named for the Native Americans who lived in that area. They were called Flatheads because of their flattened foreheads, formed by special carrying cradles they used for their young.

Flathead Lake is bordered on the east by the Swan and Mission Mountain Ranges, so the west shore offers an impressive backdrop of snow-capped peaks with brilliant blue water in the foreground.

A short drive from Flathead Lake are two major ski resorts, Mountain and Blacktail. Snowmobiling, skiing, snowshoeing and ice fishing are part of the winter fun.

One of the best parts of Flathead Lake — if you take out of your equation the other things you might love, such as wind surfing, jet skiing, kayaking and water-skiing — is the opportunity to see Wild Horse Island. Wild Horse Island is a 2,100-acre state park. Though boat access is carefully regulated, this primitive park provides the chance to see endangered palouse prairie plant species and incredible wildlife. The island is home to Rocky Mountain bighorn sheep, mule deer, songbirds, waterfowl, bald eagles, and of course wild horses.

While there are many state park campgrounds around Flathead Lake, there are ample places to stay for anyone wishing less primitive digs. Averill's Flathead Lake Lodge is one such place, with its 2,000-acre family-operated ranch. A request to Montana's Tourism Board will net information about many other accommodations. There are so many charming places, you'll want to spend time deciding on just the right one.

Another place of interest at Flathead Lake, though not a state park, bears mention. Flathead Lake Biological Station is the oldest biological research station in the United States. It was established near Bigfork in 1899 and moved to Yellow Bay in 1908. The Station Museum is a homesteader's cabin that was built in the early 1870's. Students have been coming to the station since the turn of the century.

In 1981, the Schoonover Freshwater Research Laboratory, a state-of-the-art limnological laboratory, has become one of the finest facilities in the country for freshwater research. Because the Biological Station lies within the Crown of the Continent Ecosystem, a wide variety of habitats are easily accessible from the station. Plant communities include palouse prairie grasslands, montane fir, cedar and pine forests, subalpine meadows and tundra. Water is everywhere, and aquatic ecologists will find lakes, ponds, swamps, bogs, springbrooks, streams and rivers. Four national wildlife refuges are located near the station and coupled with adjacent, remote mountains offer a home for most of the Rocky Mountain fauna, including rare species such as grizzly bear, bald eagle, and westslope cutthroat trout. The area is a photographer's paradise.

Students and faculty live in cabins scattered along the lake shoreline or in a winterized dormitory. Four laboratory buildings house the course work and research projects. Housing for up to 100 visitors is available in the summer and the facility can accommodate 30 in the winter. Long-term residences are available for researchers and visitors with families.

Because the fishing at Flathead Lake is so popular, and is open all year, it needs mentioning that not only is a Montana fishing license required, but also a tribal permit must be acquired within the Flathead

Hole in the Wall area at Judith Landing on Missouri River

Opposite: West shore of Flathead Lake

Indian Reservation. The abundant fish include lake trout, mackinaw, Dolly Varden trout, cutthroat trout, Kokanee salmon, perch, and Lake Superior whitefish.

West Shore is a park located in a mature forest of fir, pine and larch that overlooks Flathead Lake. The park's glacially-carved rock outcrops give spectacular views of Flathead Lake and the Mission and Swan mountain ranges.

If you visit Yellow Bay Park, try to do so at cherry-picking time usually in July. This little park, included in the Flathead Lake park system, is located in the heart of Montana's famous sweet cherry orchards, along Yellow Bay Creek. Another tiny, but historically significant park is Fort Owen, which is the site of the first permanent white settlement in Montana. Father Pierre DeSmet established St. Mary's Mission to minister to the Flathead Indians in 1841 and in 1850 Major John Owen established the fort as a regional trade center. Period furnishings and artifacts are displayed in the restored rooms of the east barracks. Adjacent Frenchtown Pond State Park also offers day lodging.

Splendid sunsets can be found at Lake Mary Ronan Park, a 76-acre park nestled in Douglas fir and western larch on the east shore of Lake Mary Ronan. Bird watching, huckleberry picking, swimming and mushroom hunting add to this park's charm.

Placid Lake, Whitefish Lake, Noxon Rapids Reservoir, and Salmon Lake all offer places to stop and immerse yourself in the charm of Montana.

Gold West Country

The southwest corner of Montana is a palate of mountains, broad valleys, fabled rivers, and stunning lakes. Spring Meadow Lake is one of the beauties. Located on the western edge of Helena, this 30-acre spring fed lake is noted for its clarity and depth. A natural trail circles the lake. Another breathtaking spot is Lost Creek Falls State Park. Lost Creek Falls cascade over a 50-foot drop to create scenery that makes this park so popular. Mountain goats, bighorn sheep, and other wildlife are often seen on the cliffs above the creek.

Montana's first and best known state park features one of the largest limestone caverns in the Northwest. Lewis and Clark Caverns State Park is naturally air conditioned, and the caves are electrically lighted and safe to visit. They are lined with stalactites, stalagmites and columns.

A self-guided nature tour above ground provides insight into the natural surroundings. Guided tours are only available May through September.

One of Montana's most popular state parks is Canyon Ferry Dam and Visitor Center. This reservoir is located 20 miles east of Helena. It serves as a critical feeding ground to support the bald eagle migration in the fall. At Riverside State Park, located below the dam, volunteers set up spotting scopes so visitors can get a close look at the raptors that frequent this area.

While the State Capitol Grounds don't resemble what we traditionally think of as state parks, the formal grounds and flower gardens are visited by thousands of people each year. This 50 acres is also home to the capitol building, the Montana Historical Society Museum, and the state office complex.

Granite Ghost Town and the ghost town of Elkhorn round out the parks in the Gold West Country. Elkhorn comprises the remnants of a silver mining boom that occurred in the 1880's. At its peak, the town's population was 2,500. Only two buildings remain. Granite Ghost Town is difficult to reach. It too, has a mining history. A high-clearance four-wheel drive is recommended if one wants to reach this ghost town. The small park preserves the "superintendent's house" and the old miners' union hall.

Yellowstone Country

If you seek a park that's different from the norm, Greycliff Prairie Dog Town should fit the bill. This lively blacktailed prairie dog community is protected and preserved through the efforts of the Nature Conservancy and the Montana Departments of Transportation and Fish, Wildlife and Parks. Interpretive displays provide insight into these wonderful little creatures.

A geographical focal point of great importance to early Native Americans as well as trappers, traders, and settlers, was the convergence point of the Jefferson, Madison, and Gallatin Rivers. This park, called Missouri Headwaters State Park is east of the town of Three Forks.

Also in Yellowstone Country is an irrigation reservoir, called Cooney Reservoir, that has become one of the most popular recreational areas in south-central Montana. Fishing, boating, and camping opportunities are abundant and the Beartooth Mountains provide the backdrop.

Bob Marshall Wilderness near Augusta

Flower Creek, Cabinet Mountain Wilderness near Libby

Custer Country

Custer Country, tucked in Montana's southeastern corner, is the home of the Crow and Northern Cheyenne Indian reservations. The terrain holds meandering rivers, rolling hills, and rugged canyons. The parks and places of interest in this "country" are plentiful.

One of the fascinating places to see is the state-protected Chief Plenty Coups Park. The site preserves the home of Plenty Coups, last chief of the Crow Indians. Plenty Coups' log house and store stand as reminder of the chief's efforts to lead the Crow to a peaceful co-existence with all people.

Medicine Rocks is another Native American site of importance. The area is a beautiful sample of sprawling eastern Montana. The site derives its name from the Native Americans' practice of traveling to the site to contact the magical spirits they believed resided among the unique sandstone rock formations.

The Pictograph Cave Complex is a park that safeguards the fascinating ancient rock paintings known as pictographs. More than 4,500 years old, the pictographs denote the history of the prehistoric hunters that lived within the three main caves. The caves were carved into the sandstone cliffs by the forces of water and wind. A paved .25-mile interpretive trail loops around the base of the cliff to provide visitors with a view of the pictographs.

Makoshika Park, site of pine and juniper-studded badland formations, also houses fossil remains of dinosaurs such as tyrannosaurus and triceratops. Scenic roads and nature trails abound. The name Makoshika, which sounds so beautiful rolling off the tongue, means "bad earth" or "badland" in Sioux.

Lake Elmo, on the outskirts of Billings, is a 64-acre reservoir popular for swimming, sail boarding, non-motorized boating, and fishing. The maximum depth of the lake is only 16 feet. Lifeguards are on duty July through mid-August. The park is 120 acres with hiking trails and special summer events.

Tongue River Reservoir is a 12-mile long reservoir nestled in the vibrant red shale, juniper canyons, and open prairies of southeastern Montana. The park is 640 acres that offers water sports, fishing and plain old relaxation.

Pirogue Island, a day-use-only park located in the Yellowstone River, can only be accessed by floaters; or, during low water, by fording a small channel with a vehicle. This island-park is sheltered by mature cottonwoods and is a perfect spot to view wildlife and to hunt for Montana moss agates. It is a haven for waterfowl, white-tailed deer, mule deer, and bald eagles. Although there are no designated hiking trails, the level site has easy access across its 269 acres.

A final historical site worth mentioning in "Custer Country" is the site of the June 17, 1876 battle between the Sioux and Cheyenne Indians and General Crook's infantry and cavalry — one of the largest Indian battles ever fought in the United States. It set the stage for the Indian victory eight days later when Lt. Colonel George Custer and his immediate command were wiped out at the Little Bighorn. Today, Rosebud Battlefield preserves a portion of the rolling eastern Montana prairie. Park advisors have one admonishment — watch out for rattlesnakes!

St. Mary Falls, Glacier National Park

A Peek at Montana's National Parks, Forests, and Protected Areas

While it would take volumes to thoroughly cover the depth of these riches of Montana, a slice of the most popular will whet the appetite of anyone who loves the outdoors.

Yellowstone National Park

Yellowstone National Park is only a portion of the area known as Greater Yellowstone. It encompasses 14 million acres, making it the largest temperate ecosystem in the world that remains essentially intact. The park itself, which is larger than the states of Rhode Island and Delaware combined, is actually only 16 percent of the total land mass that makes up Greater Yellowstone. The Beartooth Mountains anchor the northeast corner, while the Jefferson, the Gallatin, and the Madison, along with several mountain ranges, fill the middle. To the south, it reaches the grasslands of the Wyoming plains and the headwaters of the Colorado River system. The Continental Divide forms a backbone and the Tetons cross its middle. The Greater Yellowstone is an ecosystem in the most fundamental sense of the word. Its importance to animals and habitat preservation can't be overstated. Yellowstone is the greatest wildlife sanctuary in the United States.

Yellowstone is the oldest and largest national park in the United States, stretching not only into Montana, but also northwestern Wyoming and extending into eastern Idaho. It covers a lot of territory, with boundaries that hold 3,468.5 square miles of central Rocky Mountain land that is best known for its geysers, hot springs, canyons and waterfalls. The Yellowstone River traverses the region from south to north, flowing into Yellowstone Lake and then through the Grand Canyon. The river's passage into the canyon has created two spectacular falls. In the heart of the park is a broad plateau surrounded by rugged mountain ranges of spectacular beauty.

The geysers and hot springs have long taken top-billing because of their uniqueness. With over 10,000 geysers and hot springs and other thermal features, the park has the greatest concentration of such phenomena in the world. One added attraction to the fascination here is that the minerals in the water

White Cliff area near Big Sandy on the Missouri River

White Rock and Missouri River

have been deposited on the ground for centuries, building up brilliantly colored cones and terraces.

It seems that anything one seeks is here: fishing, boating, driving, hiking, horseback riding, bird and wildlife watching, biking, stagecoach rides, boat and bus tours, cross-country skiing, snowshoeing, and interpretive and campfire programs.

The park is always open, though access to some of the high-snowfall areas may be closed during the winter months. Even in winter, thousands of visitors travel in the park by heated snow coaches that are operated by a variety of visitor centers, lodges, and winter activities are available.

Gallatin National Forest

Snow peaks, alpine meadows, and scenic canyons are the bone structure of Gallatin National Forest. Gallatin contains about 2,151,170 acres of National Forest land and 388,000-plus acres of private land. The divided ownership is a result of land grants made to the railroads around the turn of the century, when incentives were needed for settlement of the West.

The main forest area lies south of Bozeman in two land blocks that border Yellowstone National Park. These blocks encompass the Gallatin, Madison, Absaroka, and Beartooth mountain ranges. About 41 percent of the Gallatin is designated wilderness area. One of these areas is called the Absaroka-Beartooth Wilderness and it is a slice of the Gallatin that equals 581,000 acres; the second is the Lee Metcalf Wilderness and it takes another slice of 140,594 acres (over 100,000 acres of this wilderness lie outside the Gallatin). About two percent of the Gallatin is made up of the Cabin Creek Wildlife Recreation Management Area, which is an area devoted to roadless recreation and wildlife resources.

Within Gallatin, there are more than 2,200 miles of trails, including seven National Recreation Trails, so it's a hiker's paradise. Dozens of trailheads line each side of Bridger Range. Timbered valleys and steep ridges are characteristic of the Gallatin Range, where peaks rise to 10,000 feet and petrified wood is commonly found. The Absarokas are defined by stratified volcanic and metamorphic rocks, rugged peaks, and forested valleys. The Madison Range, shaped by alpine glaciation, is a land of steep rugged peaks, knife-sharp ridges and lakes surrounded by alpine meadows. Dramatically different from all, in a land where "rugged" is a matter of degrees, are the Beartooths, which are considered to be the most rugged mountains in Montana.

Big Hole National Battlefield

In 1877, about 750 non-treaty Nez Perce fled Idaho when the Army demanded that all Nez Perce move onto a reservation a fraction of the size of their traditional homeland. In early August, after six weeks of flight and conflict, the Nez Perce stopped to camp for several days along the North Fork of the Big Hole River. They knew they had crossed into Montana Territory and believed they were safe from further pursuit. Just before daybreak, however, on August 9, they were attacked as they slept. The warriors quickly mounted a resistance and drove the military to a wooded hill nearby. The soldiers dug trenches for protection, but the Nez Perce warriors surrounded the hill and held the soldiers there. Meanwhile, the older men, women and children buried the dead and fled again.

The Battle of the Big Hole lasted less than 36 hours, yet casualties were high. Between 60 and 90 Nez Perce men, women, and children were killed, most in the initial attack on the sleeping camp. Twenty-two soldiers, a civilian guide, and five civilian volunteers were killed, and 39 more were wounded.

From the Big Hole, the Nez Perce continued to flee from the military, traveling east through Yellowstone National Park, then turning northward and moving toward the Canadian border. Several skirmishes occurred with federal troops in the weeks that followed the Battle of the Big Hole, when, finally in October the Army succeeded in forcing most of the non-treaty Nez Perce to surrender.

The Visitor Center at the park houses a small museum. Visitors are encouraged to take self-guided walks through the battlefield from sunrise to sunset. Regularly scheduled ranger-guided tours are available daily during the summer.

Glacier National Park

Glacier National Park is a land carved by prehistoric ice rivers. Beauty dots the terrain in the form of alpine meadows, waterfalls, deep forests, and about 50 glistening glaciers and 200 pristine lakes. Relatively few miles of road exist, therefore preserving the primitive beauty. Archaeological surveys in this area have found evidence of human use dating back 10,000 years. Perhaps these people were ancestors of the Native Americans that live in this area today. By the time the first European explorers came to this region, several different tribes inhabited the area. Today, the Blackfeet Reservation adjoins

Mission Mountains near Arlee

Montana mountain goat

Chief Mountain, Glacier National Park

the east side of the park. The Salish and Kootenai reservation is southwest of Glacier. The entire area holds great spiritual importance to the Blackfeet, Salish, and Kootenai people.

Around the turn of the century, people started to recognize that the value of the spectacular beauty of the area outweighed the mineral value. Facilities for tourists began to spring up. In the late 1890's, visitors could get off a train at the area that is now West Glacier and take a stagecoach ride a few miles to Lake McDonald. From there, they could take a boat ride for an 8-mile trip to the Snyder Hotel. There were no roads in the mountains, but the lakes allowed for boat travel. Soon, people like George Bird Grinnell, who was an early explorer of this area, began to push for the creation of a national park. In 1900, the area was made a Forest Preserve, but was left open to mining and homesteading. Grinnell and others worked hard to obtain the extra protection that the designation "national park" would bring. In 1910, President Taft finally signed the bill that established Glacier as the country's 10th national park.

The increasing number of visitors made the need for roads, hotels, and trails urgent. The Great Northern Railway built a number of small backcountry lodges and hotels. Visits to the park during that time would typically entail arrival by train, followed by a multi-day journey on horseback. Each day the travelers would stay in a different hotel or lodge after their long ride. The lack of roads meant visitors had to hike or ride a horse if they wanted to see the interior of the park. Soon, the need for a road brought about the building of the Going-to-the-Sun Road.

Even today, visitors marvel at what an undertaking it was to develop this road. The final section, over Logan Pass, took 11 years of work. The road itself is considered an engineering feat and, as such, has been designated a National Historic Landmark. It is one of the most, if not *the* most, scenic roads in North America.

Across the border from Glacier is Canada's Waterton Lakes National Park. In 1931, members of the Rotary Clubs of Alberta and Montana suggested joining the two parks as a symbol of the peace and friendship between our countries. In 1932, the governments decided to designate the parks as Waterton-Glacier International Peace Park, the world's first. More recently, the parks have received two other international honors. The parks are both designated Biosphere Reserves, and were named a World Heritage Site in 1995, highlighting the importance and the recognition of this area, not only by Canada and the United States, but by the world.

Visitors can still take horseback rides like early adventurers and can even stay in some of the hotels and chalets built by the Great Northern Railway. These activities can by supplemented with hiking, backpacking, sightseeing, biking, excursion boat cruises, fishing, cross-country skiing, snowshoeing, picnicking, camping, and enjoying interpretive exhibits and programs. The star attraction is the Rockies themselves with their stunning peaks and landforms. The streams, lakes, and rivers, too, are worthy destinations. Because of the geographic location and geologic history, Glacier National Park contains an exceptionally rich biological diversity of plant and animal species. This combination of spectacular scenery, diverse flora and fauna, and relative isolation from major population centers has combined to make Glacier National Park the center of one of the largest and most intact ecosystems in North America.

The wildlife here includes bighorn sheep, mountain goats, elk, grizzly bear, moose, wolves, black bear, and whitetail and mule deer. Also present are beaver, hoary marmot, river otter, marten and pika. Prevalent birds include osprey, ptarmigan, golden eagle, Clark's nutcracker, harlequin duck, and the bald eagle. Nature studies are often conducted by park rangers.

There are numerous lodging and activity choices surrounding the park. Glacier Raft Company is just one of dozens of operators that offer exploration and lodging packages.

National Bison Range

Teddy Roosevelt and the American Bison Society established the National Bison Range in 1908 with the purpose of maintaining a representative herd of American bison or buffalo. Today, this 18,541-acre refuge north of Missoula contains an assortment of big-game wildlife, including white-tailed deer, mule deer, bighorn sheep, pronghorn, elk, and mountain goats. In 1921, the added designation as a protected area for native birds was put in place. Like all of Montana, the scenery here is sensational, with the broad Flathead Valley to the north and the Mission Mountains to the east.

For birders, the short loop through the park, known as Buffalo Prairie Drive, offers the chance to see gray partridge, mourning doves, mountain bluebird, vesper sparrow, western meadowlark, and grasshopper sparrow. Along the corridor of Mission Creek birds such as the great horned owl, northern pygmy-owl, long-eared owl, and northern saw-whet owl reside. During the right season bird watchers can also spot double-crested cormorant, common merganser, belted kingfisher, western kingbird,

McDonald Valley, Glacier National Park

Opposite: Swiftcurrent Pass, Bullhead Lake

eastern kingbird, northern rough-winged swallow, marsh wren, common yellowthroat, and Townsend's solitaire. The long loop, a 19-mile drive on Red Sleep Mountain Scenic Drive, provides an opportunity to see outstanding scenery and wildlife. This loop begins in the grasslands and meadowlark and vesper sparrow are the predominant species, though mountain bluebird and dusky flycatcher can also be found. Along Pauline Creek, yellow-breasted chat and MacGillivray's warbler are the most visible species, though Lazuli bunting, yellow warbler, Wilson's warbler, red-eyed vireo, northern oriole, and dusky flycatcher can often be viewed. On the edge of the timber you will find warbling vireo, Cassin's finch, chipping sparrow, dark-eyed junco, yellow-rumped warbler and mountain chickadee. At the Bitterroot Trail rest stop you may see Clark's nutcracker, Lewis' woodpecker, northern flicker and pygmy nuthatch. At High Point, golden eagle, red-tailed hawk and rock wren can be found.

Two other birding areas are worth mentioning. The Ravalli Potholes can often, depending upon the water level, provide a stop-over for migrating birds. Tundra swan are often sighted. The other area is Jocko River Fishing Access Site. Cottonwood and dense shrubs establish the comfortable cover that Black-capped Chickadee, Red-breasted Nuthatch, and Pileated Woodpecker enjoy.

Ninepipe National Wildlife Refuge

Built around an existing irrigation reservoir on the Flathead Indian Reservation, this refuge was established in 1921. The landscape is an ancient glacial moraine pocked with thousands of potholes or "kettle ponds." The potholes formed when masses of ice in the glacial moraine melted out and left water-filled holes in the ground. The resulting abundance of ponds make Ninepipe one of the most important wetland areas in western Montana. The jagged Mission Mountains reach the sky along the eastern horizon of Ninepipe. The richness of bird watching opportunities here are almost beyond imagination. Many, many species that can't be found in the National Bison Range can be found here. Combined, the two areas hold more varieties of birds than any other area in the United States.

Rivers, Rivers, Everywhere

The Madison, approximately 70 miles long, may take the prize as most popular and most famous river in the West. The big river supports perhaps more fishermen than trout, but fishermen say you could fish any one section of the river for a year and still not know it fully. There are dozens of local guides available. Floating the river is quite popular, too. The upper river can be handled by beginners, although there are a few boulders and the current is swift. The lower river is great for white water rafters and kayakers.

For beauty, it's hard to compare any river with the Missouri. Not everyone has had kind things to say, however. Rivers were Montana's first highways and this was said about the Missouri: "Of all the variable things in creation, the most uncertain are the action of a jury, the state of a woman's mind, and the condition of the Missouri River." It was the frontier's main highway, 2,714 miles long from its source in Montana to its meeting place with the Mississippi a few miles above St. Louis, and for the largest part of that distance, it was navigable. Boats of all kinds were used, but preferred travel was by steamboat.

A portion of the Missouri is now designated as a National Wild and Scenic River. It stretches 149 miles from historic Fort Benton to the Fred Robinson Bridge on the west end of the Charles M. Russell National Wildlife Refuge. The entire Missouri Breaks area, a wildland complex of 407,492 acres is one magnificent 160-mile west-to-east wilderness separated into 21 roadless areas, bound together by the common thread of the wild Missouri River. The Missouri can be deceiving, for if you stand on the cultivated bench lands above the Missouri, you wouldn't have a clue as to the presence of the wild breaks below. Then too, immersed in the breaks, you can feel cut off from the world. With its striking rock formations and diverse flora and fauna, this river corridor includes numerous historical and archeological sites.

Swan River is the site of the Bigfork Whitewater Festival in mid-May. Prizes are awarded for those who compete and win on this Class II to V river. It's an event that organizers strive to keep fun without the main focus being the competition.

The 90-mile Gallatin River begins in the snowy peaks of the Gallatin and Madison mountain ranges. It can be a great river to float and fish, but the East Gallatin fork is often too low to float by midsummer.

Holland Lake near the town of Swan Lake

Meadowlark, the state bird

Garden Wall, Glacier National Park

Like all the rivers of Montana, the scenery surrounding the river is magnificent.

The Clark Fork River, 200 miles in length, carries more water than any other river in Montana and is one of the state's most popular floating rivers.

The Yellowstone River is still the longest free-flowing undammed waterway in the lower 48 states. Its 678-mile course takes it through southwest Montana, traveling, like all Montana rivers, through stunning terrain.

The Smith, with its limited public access, offers 60 miles of some of the finest country in Montana. Cool, deep pools snuggle up against 1,000-foot vertical cliffs of limestone. Exploring the Smith is a chance to wake up your soul.

If you were to make it a point only to explore Montana's rivers and lakes, you would see incredible visual richness that you would never forget. There are too many rivers and lakes to begin to pay tribute to all here: the Flathead Wild and Scenic River; and Flathead Lake, the largest natural freshwater lake west of the Mississippi; Clark Fork River; Red Rock Lakes; Spanish Lakes; Wolverine Lakes; the Kootenai; Stillwater River; Henry's Fork of the Snake; Fire Hole; the Smith; and the Gibbon — to mention just a few.

Bighole Valley, Bitterroot Range

The Bridger Range near Wilsall

Chinese Wall, Bob Marshall Wilderness

The Smith River near Ulm

Trapper Peak, Selway Bitterroot Wilderness

Elk Lake, Red Rock Lakes National Wildlife Reserve near Lakeview

Opposite: Emigrant Peak, Absaroka Beartooth Wilderness

Bighorn River and Canyon near Warren

Montana bighorn sheep

Bighorn River Canyon

Montana mule deer

Pryor Mountains near Warren

Opposite: Bighorn Canyon in Crow Reservation near St. Xavier

Martin Peak, Paradise Valley

Yellowstone River, Paradise Valley

Bannack State Park

Fragile prickly pear cactus

Mammoth Hot Springs, Yellowstone National Park

Charles M. Russell National Wildlife Refuge at Hell Creek Bay near Jordan

Montana grizzly bear

Colorful Characters

Montana seems to have an abundance of characters — some might say, with tongue in cheek, more now than ever before. Yet history holds some hard-to-match personalities.

Perhaps the most unbelievable was John Johnson, also known as Liver-Eating Johnson. He was a mountain man who came to this land in 1846, built a cabin for himself and his Flathead Indian wife, and tried to live peacefully. One day he returned to his cabin to find that the Crow Indians had killed his wife. He swore vengeance and went about finding it in a bloody way. It was calculated that he killed about 300 Crow and ate at least a bite of each of their livers. Later in life, he became a friend of the Crow. He also served as the first town marshal of Red Lodge when it was a new coal-mining town. It is said that there were men who were still afraid of him even after his death.

More genteel, certainly, was a cowboy named Charles Marion Russell. Charley, as he was affectionately called, came to Montana from Missouri in 1880, when he was about 16 years old. He herded sheep for a while, then became a cowboy. He was always drawing or painting pictures of cowboys and Indians. When he was in his early thirties, he married a girl named Nancy Cooper who became his business manager. He was only 23 years old when he painted Montana's most famous picture. He herded cattle during the terrible winter of 1886-1887 when stockmen lost most of their herds. Both men and animals suffered, so when asked for a report by his boss, Charley got out his watercolors and answered with a picture. The picture was the size of a postcard and it showed a gaunt cow about to collapse in the snow, with five wolves waiting for her to die. Charley Russell went on to write and illustrate several books. The personal letters he wrote to friends are museum prizes now, because he illustrated even his letters.

Although she didn't spend all of her time in Montana, Calamity Jane spent too much of her time there as far as Montana citizens were concerned. She told so many lies about herself that nobody was sure where the facts stopped and the fiction began. Her real name was Martha Jane Canarray (maybe, stories differ because of her evasiveness). She said she was born in Missouri in 1848, but maybe it was 1844. In any case, she came with her parents to Virginia City, Montana as a teenager. She dressed like a man, smoked nasty black cigars, swore, and drank as if there was no tomorrow. She was skilled with a 30-foot bullwhip, often made her living by chopping down pine trees to make fence posts, and she served as camp cook for a bunch of horse thieves. What she claimed she had done was even more spectacular. She claimed she had been a stagecoach driver, a pony express rider, and a scout for General Custer. She said her nickname came from an Army captain who told her after she saved his life that she was a wonderful woman to have around in a calamity. She claimed later that she was actually in the Army at the time, but it can only be verified that she was in the Army once or twice as a civilian teamster, driving mules.

Despite her roughness, she had a good heart, for she marched in and took care of families, nursing and cleaning for them when smallpox struck and no one else would care for them for fear of contracting the disease. She married once or twice and had at least two children. The love of her life was Wild Bill Hickok, the famous gunslinger and gambler. She claimed she married him, but the facts show that the daughter she claimed was his was born three years before she met him . . . not to mention that he already had a wife. Nonetheless, her devotion to Hickok was clear. She claimed she brutally murdered the man who shot him in the back while he was playing poker, but that was another of her tall tales.

In her later years, Calamity was often arrested for shooting at stranger's feet, or shooting up a saloon. In 1902, the year before she died, she took after a Billings, Montana store clerk with an ax. She's buried by the man she loved, Wild Bill Hickok, as this was her final request.

Today the folks of Montana aren't perhaps quite as colorful as Calamity and her ilk, but they remain a highly independent, free-thinking people. The population is about 879,000 with 53 percent of the people living in urban areas. The largest cities are Billings, Great Falls, Missoula, Helena, and Bozeman.

Makoshika State Park near Glendive

Beartooth Pass, Absaroka Beartooth Wilderness near Red Lodge

A City Here and There

The Western Region

The western region of the state includes the towns of Kalispell, Missoula, Whitefish, and Hamilton. Kalispell has a population of about 12,000. From there you can strike out in about any direction and run into stunning country, such as Flathead Lake and its surroundings. On the shore of Flathead Lake lies Bigfork, a town inundated with art galleries, gift shops and bookstores. South of Flathead Lake lies the Mission Valley, and the dramatic Mission Mountains. North of Kalispell is the lively town of Whitefish, with its ticket to fame being the ski area called Big Mountain.

Missoula holds title of third largest city, with its population of 45,000. It is considered the transportation hub of western Montana, and is an excellent jumping-off point for exploring this part of the state. It is also site of the University of Montana. As with all of Montana, recreational opportunities abound. Missoula's two ski areas are worth mentioning because of their unparalleled skiing. Snowbowl has been written up by several ski magazines because of its 30 runs and 2,600-foot vertical drop. Marshall Mountain Ski Resort, only six miles from Missoula, has over 480 acres of scenery and winter recreational opportunities.

South of Missoula lies the Bitterroot Valley, with its largest town being Hamilton (population 5,000). The Sapphire Mountains guard the east, the Bitterroots the west, and the Bitterroot River flows between them. The Bitterroot Valley is often billed as "hiker's heaven."

The North Central Area

Located on the spot where Lewis and Clark were forced to spend nearly a month, Great Falls is Montana's second largest city, with a population of about 55,000. Unfortunately, the falls that caused the explorers so much trouble are now harnessed with dams to provide hydroelectric power. Charles Russell, the famous cowboy artist, spent many productive years in this town and his home, log cabin art studio, and 7,500 of his works are preserved here in the C. M. Russell Museum.

The second-largest city in this area is Havre, population 10,000. Havre, Great Falls, and Cut Bank form the corners of Montana's "Golden Triangle" — the most productive wheat and barley farming land in the state, contributing more than 50 percent of the state's grain.

The third largest town in the North Central area is Lewistown (about 6,000 population). It is the commercial center for the Judith Basin, a productive farming and ranching area.

The South Central Area

Helena got its start when four ex-Confederate soldiers struck gold in a place they called "Last Chance Gulch." In 1875, it became the territorial capital, and then in 1894 became the new capital of Montana. Helena offers many attractions for her visitors, including the State Capitol itself, the Montana Historical Society, the beautiful Cathedral of St. Helena, and much more.

The historic town of Deer Lodge is a short distance from Helena. Though many Montana towns got their start as mining camps, Deer Lodge started out as the headquarters of Montana's first cattle ranch, and the ranch itself is now a national historic site. The Old Montana Prison Complex and the Towe Ford Collection are other sites to see in Deer Lodge.

Butte, where copper was king, was a miner's town. At one time, when the copper boom was on, Butte had a population of more than 100,000. Today, that population has dropped to around 33,000 and the city has the chore of cleaning up the results of its mining legacy.

Twenty-five miles west of Butte is another copper town, Anaconda, where the tallest smelter in North America was built. The smelter, built from nearly 7 million bricks, is now a monument. A natural monument lies nearby, in Lost Creek State Park, where limestone cliffs, granite formations, and waterfalls are the stars.

South of Butte you can find some of Montana's best farming and ranching country, including the Big Hole and the Beaverhead Valley. ("Hole" is western for "valley.") The center of commerce here is Dillon. The Big Hole Battlefield National Monument is close by.

The third largest city in this area is Bozeman, with a population of around 22,000. Montana State University is here, as is the Museum of the Rockies, and the American Computer Museum. About an hour

Stubby Point, Fort Peck Lake near Brockway

Beautiful wheat field, Tobacco Root Mountains near Harrison

south of Bozeman is Big Sky, home to the state's premier downhill skiing resort. During the summer, Big Sky is close to fabulous rafting fun on the Gallatin River.

The Eastern Area

Livingston, Billings, Red Lodge, Miles City, Jordan, and Fort Peck are the mainstays of this area. While Billings is by far the largest city in Montana, the others are spots in the road population-wise. Billings, at a population of over 100,000, has almost an eighth of the total population of the state. It's been dubbed the "Midland Empire" because it is the trading center for not only eastern Montana, but for northern Wyoming, the western Dakotas, and parts of Canada's prairie provinces. The city is appealingly ringed with sandstone cliffs called "The Rimrocks." Southeast of Billings lie the Pictograph Caves State Monument. Billings is also home to the only zoo in Montana and has other points-of-interest such as the Western Heritage Center and the Yellowstone Art Center that can make a stop in the city worthwhile.

South of Billings is the small town of Red Lodge, billed by *Men's Journal* as one of "America's 25 Coolest Mountain Towns." "Red Lodge is still a genuine frontier town — a little more than a mile up, and all but hidden in the rugged folds of the incredible Beartooth Range." A trip to visit the town is, in itself, a treat because of the Beartooth Scenic Byway that was built in 1936. The town offers every imaginable kind of outdoor recreation, including skiing at nearby Red Lodge Mountain Ski Area.

Miles City hosts the Range Riders Museum, with an authentic one-room schoolhouse, a frontier cabin, a sheep wagon, and an officer's quarters — the only remaining building from nearby Fort Keogh. It also houses an outstanding collection of artifacts from the settling of the West.

Wide-open spaces is what you get if you travel the northeast corner of Montana, for there are three towns that have the only gas pumps in 300 miles — Circle, Jordan, and Grassrange. Cattle and sheep are the primary inhabitants. North of Jordan is Fort Peck Lake, which was created when the Fort Peck Dam was built in the 1930's. There's a small museum at the powerhouse at Fort Peck Dam. Some of the fossils uncovered during construction of the dam are displayed. Be careful if it rains around here, for the dirt roads in this part of Montana can become so slippery that even the best of four-wheel drives have a hard time getting around.

Ghost Towns to Explore

Virginia City — Montana, that is, not to be confused with the Nevada town — is the best-preserved Gold Rush town anywhere in the West. Its strike-it-rich history began when six prospectors stumbled upon the bounty of the world's richest deposit of placer gold. After this discovery at Alder Gulch, the boom began. It took it only a year to fizzle and for most of the population to abandon town. By 1945, although a few old-timers had hung on, plans were in the works to tear it down and sell it for firewood. Sue and Charles Bovey, wealthy ranchers from Great Falls, Montana with a penchant for history, decided that shouldn't be the course for this little landmark. They bought up much of the town and set about restoring it to its former glory. It was a 50-year devotion, which grew to take in nearby Nevada City. The financial drain eventually became too much and the family sold the sites to the state of Montana. The town's business district included more than 50 original buildings that were erected in the 1860's and 1870's. You can see where the state's first newspaper, the *Montana Post*, was printed in 1864 or cross the street to see the Wells Fargo and Company Express Office. The Kiskadden Barn and Blacksmith, host to some of Montana's best vigilante parties, is down the street. The town's greatest asset is that these places are the real thing, not carefully constructed look-alikes built solely to lure tourists.

Bannack State Park is another spot for history buffs, with more than 50 preserved buildings that were once the site for the gold-mining town of Bannack.

Not a spot where visitors have been encouraged, Comet is nonetheless a town where history speaks out. Records of the first mining activity in this town are, perhaps purposely, hazy. The current town consists of run-down buildings including a boarding house, mill superintendent's home, livery stable, and the giant mine of the Basin Montana Tunnel Company. The town had 22 saloons at one time. At Rosie's Boardinghouse, miners could obtain room and board for 75 cents a day, with money left over from their daily average wage of $3.90 to visit the "soiled doves" in the nearby parlor houses, or throw back a few shots of "pop skull." The town even had a schoolhouse with about 20 students at any given time. The town has been highly vandalized, so much of the material that contributes to its historical value is, sadly, disappearing.

Montana winter bison

Pompey's Pillar near Billings

Opposite: The Gallatin River near Big Sky

South of Helena lies the ghost town of Elkhorn. The buildings are fascinating, from the false-fronted, balconied Fraternity Brothers Hall, to the Grand Hotel, to the saloons. The "real" West is evident in bullet marks and even in the tiny cemetery perched high above the town, where marble lambs atop children's grave markers tell of the diphtheria epidemic which claimed the lives of many.

Garnet, named for the semi-precious stone found there, is an impressive little ghost town. Like most of the mining towns, it's in the high country so the weight of countless winter snows have played havoc, yet there are still some buildings in relatively good condition. The ads in the *Garnet Mining News* tell the story of the town, with everything from insurance agents offering to "draw up bonds, leases and deeds or other legal papers," to E.C. Lewis, proprietor of the Mascot Saloon, proclaiming "Just Opened, With Everything New, Clean, and Bright." Mrs. Lydia E. Pinkham's Vegetable Compound was also touted as the ideal French tonic for body and brain, claiming children needed to put it in their blood "for proper condition for spring's changeable weather" — buy it at Moore's Revealed Remedy. Five drops were claimed to be "The Pleasantest, Most Powerful and Effective Never-failing Remedy for Rheumatism, Sciatica, Neuralgia, LaGrippe and Catarrh." There were about 50 mines in the area, including the famous Nancy Hanks, which produced about $960,000 in ore during its peak year in 1896.

There are places everywhere in Montana where perhaps a few bricks mark the last physical presence of a grand dance hall or a mining flume clings to a hillside as faint evidence of the past. Still alive and present are the tales of old Montana, like that of the use of a $11,880 gold nugget put into play as a handball or of the 1,000 camels the Department of War brought in for use as pack animals.

Montana's history is as rich as her infamous beauty. For as John Steinbeck wrote in *Travels with Charley*, "I am in love with Montana. For other states, I have admiration, respect, recognition, even some affection, but with Montana, it is love."

About the Photographers

Gordon and Cathie Sullivan are blessed to live in the heart of the rugged mountains of northwest Montana. A short walk from their back door in Libby, finds them in the depth of one of Montana's most isolated wilderness areas, the Cabinet Mountains. It is this constant influence that gives them their understanding of the natural beauty and geographic diversity reflected in their photographs of Montana.

As full time professional photographers they have dedicated their talents, skills and effort to capturing outstanding natural images. Gordon is a native of Montana who loves the high mountains. For over 25 years he has honed his skills as a wilderness enthusiast and conservationist through his career in outdoor photography.

Cathie is one of Montana's most accomplished portrait photographers. Her sincere love of the solitude and wild places brings her to locations seldom visited by other wilderness travelers. Cathie lived in Wyoming, Alaska, and Colorado before settling in the Montana mountains. Her photographic eye catches nature's best, plus the simplicity of its smallest intrinsic element.

Together this pair presents an unmatched dedication to both wilderness and spirit. It is this dedication that inspired their photographic work that ripples softly through the pages of this photo essay of their favorite state.

About the Author

Although Linda Stirling's love of Montana is not as often quoted as Steinbeck's, it's an area for which she, too, has great appreciation. "When you have a need to seek peace and pristine beauty, Montana is one of the few places left in the United States where that is possible. This is a part of the country with areas that give people a chance to see unblemished land, land that makes you feel connected to the earth in a way that few areas are able to do anymore. Montana is rightly treasured by all who inhabit her, but she is also a treasure to anyone who values the land and the preservation of it and its animal inhabitants, and in that sense she belongs to us all."

Linda Stirling is the author of several books published by Beautiful America, including *Oregon Coast*, *Idaho*, and *Columbia River Gorge*. She and her family make their home in Portland, Oregon.

Medicine Rocks State Park near Ekalaka

Back Cover: Tough-leaved iris and doe